Adventures in Lettering

Dawn Nicole Warnaar

Walter Foster Jr.

Quarto is the authority on a wide range of topics.
Quarto educates, entertains, and enriches the lives of our readers—
enthusiasts and lovers of hands-on living.
www.quartoknows.com

6 Orchard Road, Suite 100
Lake Forest, CA 92630
quartoknows.com
Visit our blogs at quartoknows.com

MIX
Paper from
responsible sources
FSC® C016973

Printed in China
1 3 5 7 9 10 8 6 4 2

TABLE OF CONTENTS

REPEAT AFTER ME:

Practice
Makes
Progress

Hello my creative friends! I'm so excited you picked up this book.
I love to see people fall in love with hand-lettering just like I have.
I want to start by giving you a little heart-to-heart pep talk.

In my time teaching lettering, I've noticed when people share their work,
they often include a disclaimer along the lines of "It's not very good but..."
Can you promise not to do that? Embrace your unique style and be
proud of your work and your progress! Truth be told, I'm not a big fan of
overly perfect art anyway. The imperfections and nuances of hand-drawn art
and lettering are what I find so very charming.

The goal of the exercises in this book is simply to provide you a space to
practice your lettering skills! We are all at different places in our creative
journeys, but every single one of us was a beginner at one point.

Most importantly, remember the mantra as we begin our
Adventures in Lettering:
Practice Makes Progress.

xoxo,

LETTERING TOOLS

To do most of the exercises in this book, all you need are the basics: pencils, an eraser, and colored pencils or markers. For some of the projects, you'll also need a few special supplies. While this book has room for you to practice, a lot of the exercises are ones you can do over and over again in your own sketch pad.

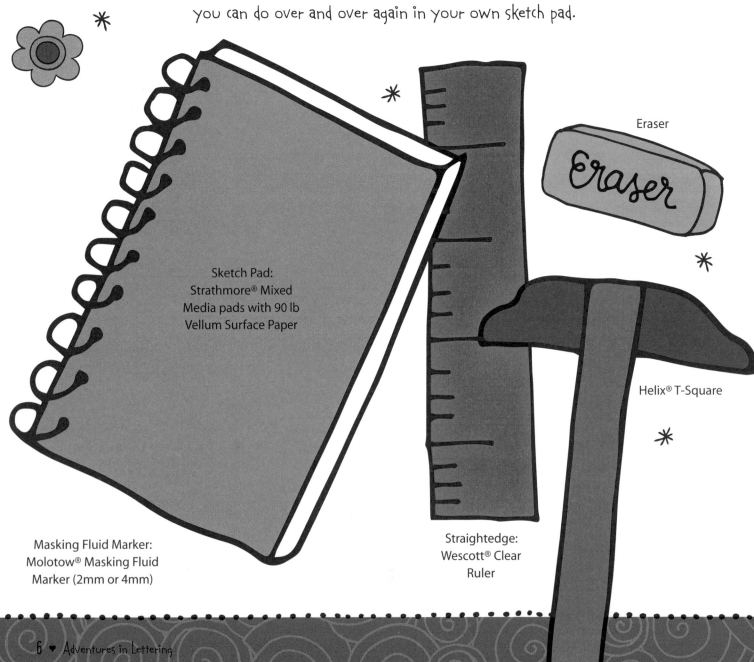

Eraser

Sketch Pad:
Strathmore® Mixed
Media pads with 90 lb
Vellum Surface Paper

Helix® T-Square

Masking Fluid Marker:
Molotow® Masking Fluid
Marker (2mm or 4mm)

Straightedge:
Wescott® Clear
Ruler

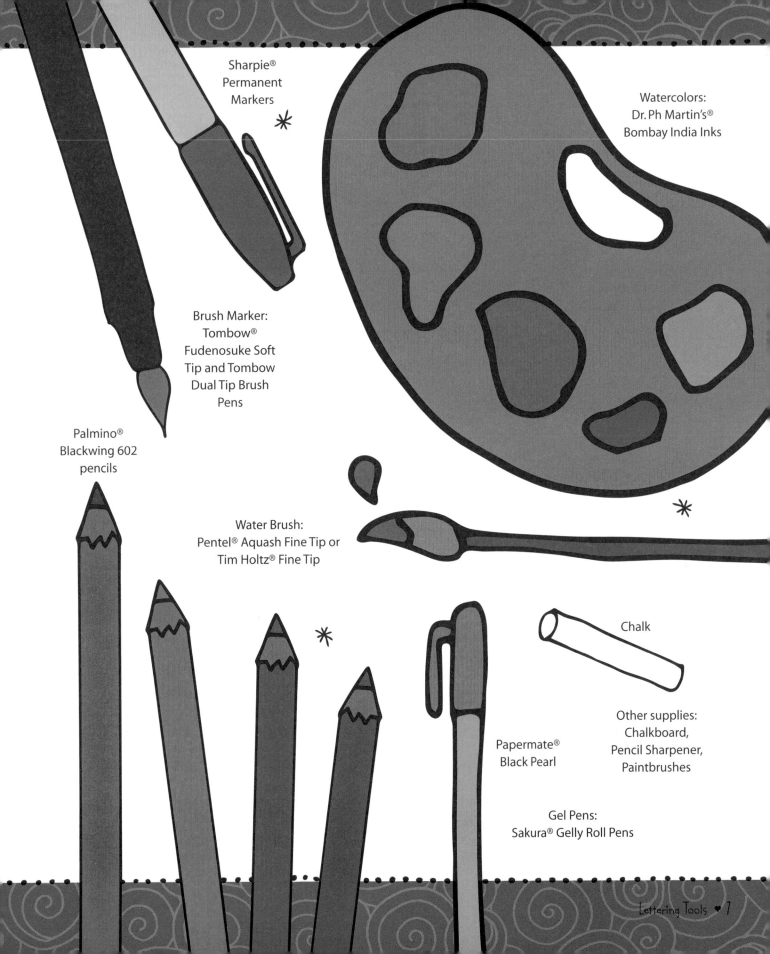

Sharpie® Permanent Markers

✳

Watercolors: Dr. Ph Martin's® Bombay India Inks

Brush Marker: Tombow® Fudenosuke Soft Tip and Tombow Dual Tip Brush Pens

Palmino® Blackwing 602 pencils

Water Brush: Pentel® Aquash Fine Tip or Tim Holtz® Fine Tip

✳

Chalk

✳

Other supplies: Chalkboard, Pencil Sharpener, Paintbrushes

Papermate® Black Pearl

Gel Pens: Sakura® Gelly Roll Pens

What is Lettering?

During my time teaching lettering, I've found people have two main hurdles that prevent them from trying hand-lettering: "bad" handwriting and being a lefty. Guess what? My handwriting is not awesome and I'm a lefty. I'm proof that you can overcome both of these hurdles and excel at hand-lettering.

For my fellow lefties, I've found that it simply means I have to put in extra practice time. That's it. Practice, practice, and more practice. And if, like me, you're not a fan of your handwriting, there's hope because hand-lettering is very different from your handwriting. And remember, imperfections are part of the charm of hand-lettering!

START WITH YOUR NAME

Let's do a simple exercise to show the difference between hand-lettering and your handwriting.

SUPPLIES:
- Sketch pad
- Pencil
- Black fine-tip marker

STEPS:

1. Print your name.

2. Write your name in script/cursive.

3. Draw your name in at least three different styles.

Print

Lettering

Cursive

Which one of these steps is lettering?

#3! Lettering is simply the art of drawing letters. If you can draw, you can letter!

TIP!

Notice how color choice and illustrations change the mood of each hand-lettered example. Which one is fun? Playful? Feminine?

FAUX CALLIGRAPHY

An easy way to understand how traditional calligraphy works is to learn faux calligraphy! With this method you'll manually create the thicker downstrokes to create lovely faux-calligraphic styles of lettering in your artwork.

SUPPLIES:
- Straightedge
- Pencil
- Eraser
- Marker

STEPS:

1. Write a word in script.

2. Add a second line to the downstroke(s) of each letter.

3. Color in the space between the original downstrokes and the line you added.

4. Add details, such as a dot at the end of any open strokes.

④

Upstroke: A stroke that goes upward.
Downstroke: A stroke that goes downward.

Your turn!

Trace over the outline and create your own faux calligraphy.

Let's Practice!

I've created an example of Faux Calligraphy on the opposite page using the quote "The only way to have a friend is to be one" by Ralph Waldo Emerson. Follow the steps below to create your own original, handmade piece of artwork!

HERE ARE THE STEPS:

1. Sketch out the quote on scrap paper to see how you like it laid out. This helps you figure out how many words per line and how many lines of text you'll have.

2. Draw guidelines for each line of text on your sketch pad using a straightedge and a pencil.

3. Sketch out the quote lightly in pencil.

4. Go over your text with a fine-point marker.

5. Thicken the downstrokes with faux calligraphy, and add any details you'd like.

6. Once dry, gently erase your pencil lines.

7. Add more color!

The only way to have a friend is to be one.

- Emerson

Brush Calligraphy Basics

Calligraphy is such a beautiful style of lettering! It requires you to use pressure to control the width of your strokes. However, using a traditional calligraphy nib can be quite the challenge. I found it was much easier to start with brush pens to learn how to use pressure to control the width of my stroke. After I became comfortable with brush calligraphy, using a traditional nib became much easier.

For now, we're going to focus on practicing basic strokes to get used to using pressure to write in a calligraphic style. It may feel awkward at first, but the more you practice, the easier and more natural it will become.

CALLIGRAPHY BASICS

- Hold your brush pen comfortably and at an angle in your hand. I find it's easiest to grip it fairly close to the nib. As you practice, you'll find exactly what grip and angle work best for you!

- Keep your brush pen at the same angle as you write. You may want to angle your paper to make this easier.

- Go super slow! Writing this way takes a lot of practice, and going super slow is the best way to get started.

LET'S PRACTICE!

SUPPLIES:

- Brush Pen Marker(s)

My favorite brush pens are the Tombow® Dual Tip Brush Pens. They'll work perfectly for this practice sheet.

- I've created a Basic Strokes practice sheet for you on the next page. I recommend photocopying it so you can use it over and over again!

- For the upstrokes, use really light pressure. Just barely kiss the page with the brush pen's nib.

- For the downstrokes, use heavy pressure by pushing down on the brush pen's nib.

TIP!

Don't be afraid of applying pressure to your brush pen's nib. These markers were made with flexible tips and were designed to be used that way!

REMEMBER: USE LIGHT PRESSURE FOR UPSTROKES AND HEAVY PRESSURE FOR DOWNSTROKES!

LINE 1: UPSTROKES

LINE 2: DOWNSTROKES

LINE 3: ALTERNATING UPSTROKES AND DOWNSTROKES

LINE 4: CIRCLES

LINE 5: LOOPS

Your turn!

Playing with Style

You may ask yourself: "How do I find my own style?"
The best way to find your style is to practice and play with letters!
Over time, your style starts to pop out at you.

This exercise is a great way to play with letters and try a lot of different styles. I chose the letter "B" and drew it as many ways as I could think of. It's okay if you don't love every style you put on paper. Just keep going until you fill your page!

SUPPLIES:

- Sketch pad
- Pencil
- Black fine-tip marker
- Colored pencils or markers

TIP!
Don't stop with just one letter. When you finish this exercise, there are 25 more letters of the alphabet you can try it with!

1. Pick a letter.

2. Draw it as many ways as you can think of (but try to do at least 10 different lettering styles).

3. Have fun playing with and creating different lettering styles!

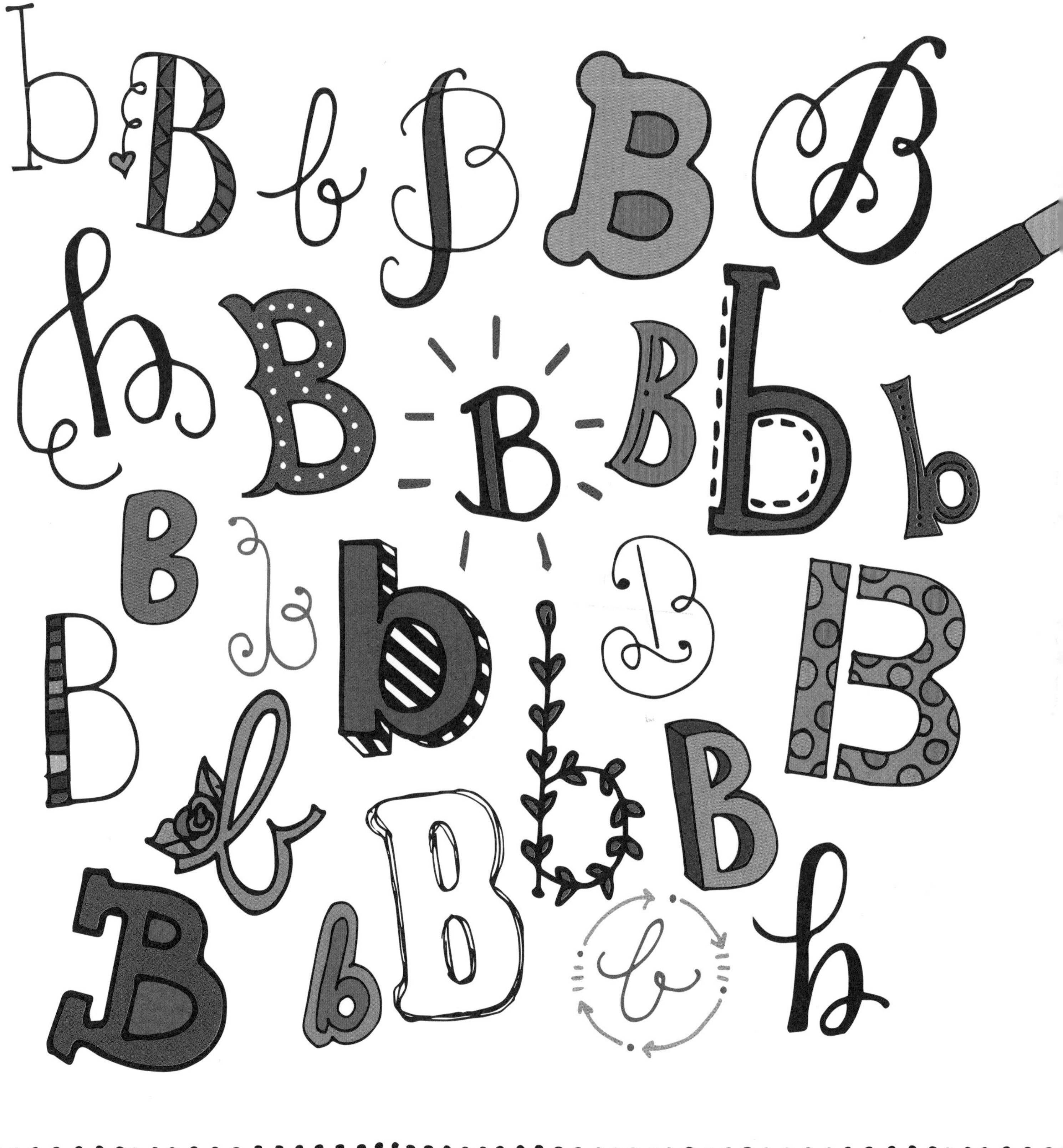

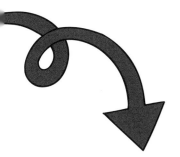

Let's Practice!

DROP CAPS

A drop cap is the first letter of a paragraph. The letter is much larger and drops down to take over part of the first few lines of text. (You often see this in books.) In this exercise, we are going to make our own drop cap.

My favorite style is the Decorative Drop Cap. I've shown you my take on a drop cap using the Thoreau quote on the opposite page.

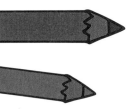

NOW LET'S PLAY WITH STYLE!

SUPPLIES:

- Sketch pad
- Pencil
- Black fine-tip marker
- Colored pencils or markers

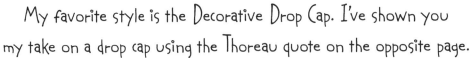

TIP!

Want some Drop Cap Inspiration? Pop over to the Internet and look up "The Daily Drop Cap" by one of my favorite lettering artists, Jessica Hische.

1. Pick a letter.

2. Draw it as a drop cap.

3. Try it with a few different letters and styles.

In the thickest darkness, the stars shine brightest.

-Thoreau

DANGLED LETTERING

Adding dangles is a great way to add character and interest to your lettering. It gives a fun, playful, and whimsical vibe to your artwork! Where to add dangles is really up to you, but try to add them in a way that keeps the overall piece balanced—if you add one to the first letter, also add one to the last letter. Can you see how I create balance in my examples?

Your turn!

SUPPLIES:

- Sketch pad
- Pencil
- Black fine-tip marker
- Colored pencils or markers

TIP!

If you love this style of lettering, be sure to check out Joanne Fink's artwork and books. She is a master of whimsical lettering and dangled designs.

1. Sketch out a word in any lettering style you like. Add dangles.

2. Once you're happy with your lettering artistry, trace with a fine-tip black marker.

3. Allow to dry, and then erase your pencil lines.

4. Add color!

TANGLED MONOGRAM

Tangling is a method of using repetitive patterns to create stunning visual works of art. In this exercise, we're going to combine a single letter (a.k.a. "monogram") with patterning techniques. This is another great way to add character and style to your hand-lettering.

NOW LET'S TANGLE!

SUPPLIES:

- Sketch pad
- Pencil
- Black fine-tip marker
- Colored pencils or markers

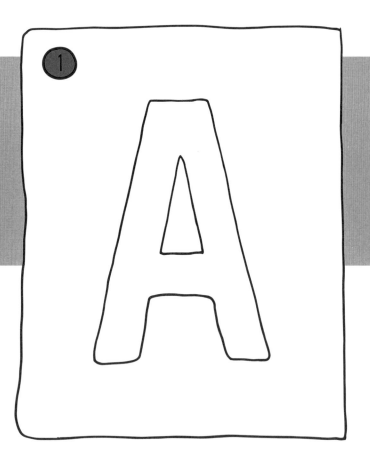

1. Draw a rectangle with a block letter inside.

2. Add a border around the block letter.

3. Add dots to the rectangle border.

4. Draw lines to create divisions in the space between the two borders.

5. Add a different pattern into each space you created with the division lines.

6. Add tangles to your block letter.

7. Add color!

ADDING ILLUSTRATION

Adding doodles and illustrations to your lettering is a great way to create your own style, character, and interest to a piece of hand-lettering art. The mix of lettering and art creates a fun and whimsical feeling.

This "All About Me" exercise is a great way to play with illustrations. Start by writing facts about yourself and things you like (or don't like). Add in illustrations and fun lettering styles wherever you like. Keep adding facts and doodles until you fill your page!

ALL ABOUT ME ACTIVITY

SUPPLIES:

- Sketch pad
- Pencil
- Black fine-tip marker
- Colored pencils or markers

1. Sketch your "All About Me" story in pencil on your page.

2. Trace with a fine-tip black marker.

3. Allow to dry, and then erase your pencil lines.

4. Add color!

ALL ABOUT ME: >Hi!< My name is dawnnicole.
I'm a DESIGNER who ♥'s coffee + DONUTS.
I ♥Love♥ to spend time doing ART and
anything CREATIVE. My husband flies
airplanes. I don't really like to >FLY.<
I'd rather take a road trip.
We have 3 KIDS and
2 DOGS. JAX LOLA If I had to pick one food
to eat for the rest of my life, I'd choose
SUSHI (yum!.yum!.). My favorite
color is aquamarine. I enjoy RUNNING,
watching TV, reading books, cooking,
and I really, really love to SLEEP! zzzz

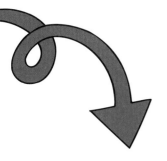

Let's Practice!

LETTERING STYLES

One of the biggest challenges my lettering students face is coming up with new styles of lettering. This section will show you various styles of lettering to spark your own creativity. For practice purposes, you can re-create my styles, but it would be even better if you try to put your own spin on them. For each style, I have given you a sample alphabet and space to practice it on your own! For the more complicated styles, I've also given you step-by-step instruction on how to create the letter style.

BASIC LETTERING STYLES

Bravo!

Sans Serif

Sans means "without." Sans serif letters do not have any little lines or curves at the ends of the letter strokes. I call this style the "modern" one.

Bravo!

Serif

Serif-style letters have little lines or curves at the end of each letter stroke. I call this the "traditional" one.

Script

Script lettering is also known as cursive. Calligraphy is a type of script font. The letters are often (but not always) connected in script lettering. I call this style the "fancy" one.

Bravo!

BRAVO!

DECORATIVE

Decorative lettering styles are what I call the "fun" ones. These might include very ornate styles or artistic styles. Some of the styles in this section are decorative: Floral Alphabet, Decorative Serif Hearts Alphabet, and Funky Doodle Alphabet.

SCRIPT ALPHABET

Aa Bb Cc Dd Ee

Ff Gg Hh Ii Jj

Kk Ll Mm Nn

Oo Pp Qq Rr Ss

Tt Uu Vv Ww

Xx Yy Zz

Your turn!

BLOCK ALPHABET

ABCDE
FGHIJK
LMNOP
QRSTU
VWXYZ

Your turn!

3D BLOCK ALPHABET

ABCDE
FGHIJK
LMNOP
QRSTU
VWXYZ

Your turn!

SERIF ALPHABET

Aa Bb Cc Dd Ee

Ff Gg Hh Ii Jj

Kk Ll Mm Nn

Oo Pp Qq Rr Ss

Tt Uu Vv Ww

Xx Yy Zz

Your turn!

FLORAL ALPHABET

ABCDE
FGHIJK
LMNOP
QRSTU
VWXYZ

Your turn!

SWIRLY ALPHABET

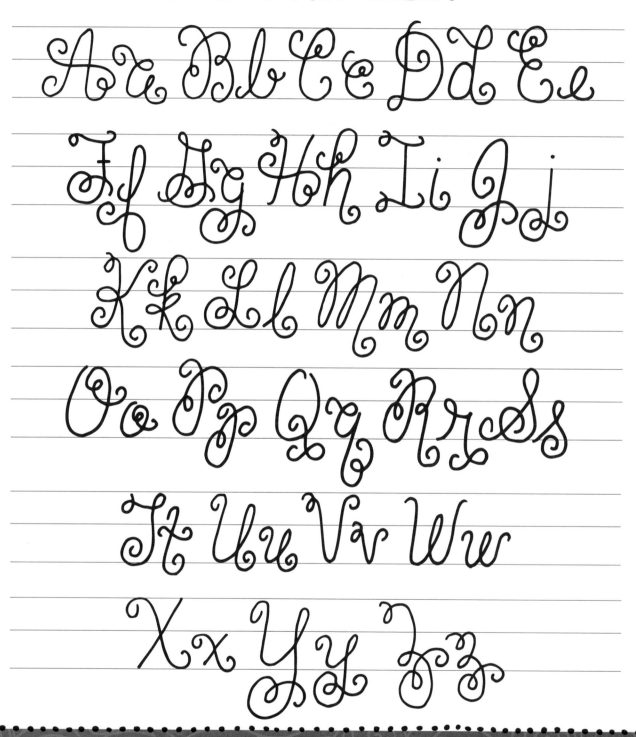

Your turn!

BUBBLE ALPHABET

A B C D E F
G H I J K
L M N O P Q
R S T U V
W X Y Z

STEP ONE

Your turn!

STEP TWO

STEP THREE

DOODLED ALPHABET

Your turn!

FAUX CALLIGRAPHY ALPHABET

Aa Bb Cc Dd Ee

Ff Gg Hh Ii Jj

Kk Ll Mm Nn

Oo Pp Qq Rr Ss

Tt Uu Vv Ww

Xx Yy Zz

Your turn!

BRUSH LETTERING UPPERCASE

A B C D E

F G H I J K

L M N O P

Q R S T U

V W X Y Z

Your turn!

BRUSH LETTERING LOWERCASE

a b c d e

f g h i j k

l m n o p

q r s t u

v w x y z

Your turn!

DECORATIVE SERIF HEART ALPHABET

ABCDE

FGHIJK

LMNOP

QRSTU

VWXYZ

Your turn!

Let's Practice!

HAND-LETTERED PROJECTS

Try out your hand-lettering skills on these fun project ideas! I've broken down each project into easy steps you can follow. This section features a range of different mediums to use to create your crafty hand-lettered designs.

RECIPE ILLUSTRATION

Who doesn't love food? I sure do! I also love mixing my love of food with
my lettering and art through a simple recipe illustration. The "Adding Illustration:
All About Me" exercise on page 30 is great prep for this project.
Pick any recipe you love, and start lettering! I went with a simple hot cocoa recipe.

SUPPLIES:

- Sketch pad
- Pencil
- Black fine-tip marker
- Colored pencils, markers, and/or watercolors

1. Roughly sketch out several ideas on scrap paper to determine the best layout. Once you determine the layout, sketch your recipe illustration in pencil. Trace with a fine-point black marker. Let dry and gently erase out your pencil lines.

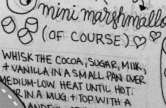

TIP!

Turn your recipe illustration into a handmade gift.

2. Add color! Watercolors, markers, and colored pencils work great.

Hot Cocoa

FOR ONE

Whisk 2 TBSP unsweetened Cocoa Powder +

1-2 TBSP sugar

A PINCH OF salt + YUM!

1 CUP MILK

¼ TSP vanilla

& A LOT OF mini marshmallows (OF COURSE)

WHISK THE COCOA, SUGAR, MILK, + VANILLA IN A SMALL PAN OVER MEDIUM-LOW HEAT UNTIL HOT. POUR IN A MUG + TOP WITH A BIG HANDFUL OF MARSHMALLOWS!

Enjoy!

CHALKBOARD ART

Chalkboard art is a classic. It's really fun to create hand-lettered art in chalk, and it's super easy to erase mistakes. Any chalkboard will work—I picked mine up at a craft store. Be sure to use regular chalk for this project because sidewalk chalk can stain chalkboards. Try to mix some of the lettering exercises and styles from sections one and two into your chalk art! If you want your work to be permanent, use paint markers instead of chalk.

NOW LET'S DO SOME CHALK ART!

SUPPLIES:
- Scrap paper
- Ruler or T-square
- Pencil sharpener
- Chalkboard
- Chalk in white and assorted colors
- Paper towels or a rag
- Cotton swabs (for erasing)

1. If your chalkboard is new like mine, you'll need to prep it. Simply rub a sideways piece of chalk over the whole board, and then erase it with a rag or paper towel. This will prevent your drawings from getting "burned" into the chalkboard, so you can re-use it over and over for new designs.

2. As always, sketch your layout ideas on scrap paper. Once you're happy with your layout, move to the chalkboard and draw your lettering.

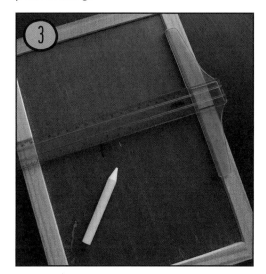

3. Sharpen your chalk with the pencil sharpener, re-sharpening your pieces often as you work. I like to use my ruler to mark the center point of my chalkboard and letter from the center. For this project, I started with "to who" and lettered from the center out. This will help keep your work evenly spaced.

TIP!

You can use a free photo-editing program like Picasa® to crop the photo of your work and make a print to frame, gift, or even sell!

4. After you're happy with your lettering, add some details and color! Before you erase and try something new, take photos of your work so you always have it!

MIRROR CARDS

I love using inspirational messages in my work. It's always nice to surround yourself with positive sayings and reminders. Stick these mirror cards on your mirror, on your walls, or even your locker, if you have one. You can also make a bunch of these mirror cards—or "Kindness cards"—and hand them out to family and friends who might need a little note of encouragement. For this project, we'll be working on our brush calligraphy skills.

TIP!
Remember, light pressure for the upstroke and heavy pressure for the downstroke. Can you see how the tip bends in the downstroke image?

NOW LET'S MAKE SOME MIRROR CARDS!

SUPPLIES:

- Smooth white card stock or unlined index cards
- Bright card stock
- Paper friendly glue or tape
- Pencil
- Eraser
- Brush calligraphy pen with a small nib (tip). (I used a Tombow® Fudenosuke Soft Tip.)

1. Cut your white card stock down to 3" x 5" inches. Cut your bright card stock slightly larger so it will form a border when you glue them together. Sketch your phrases on your white card stock in pencil, and then trace with the brush calligraphy pen. Once it's dry, gently erase your pencil lines.

2. Glue lettered cards to the bright card stock. Tape to your mirror, or anywhere else the positive message will brighten your day!

LETTERING WITH MASKING FLUID

Masking fluid is such a fun medium to work with. It comes in a variety of forms, but the easiest way to work with it for lettering is to use a masking fluid marker. I love the Molotow® Grafx Art Masking Liquid Pump Marker in the 2mm tip size. You can find these markers at your local craft store, usually in the fine arts painting section.

SUPPLIES:

- Watercolor paper (I use cold-pressed Canson® Watercolor 140-lb.)
- Masking fluid marker
- Pencil
- Eraser
- Watercolors
- Paintbrush (a mop brush works really well for this project)
- Kraft paper (optional)

1. Pick a phrase and sketch it lightly in pencil on your watercolor paper.

2. On scrap paper, depress the tip of your masking fluid marker until the fluid starts to flow. Then move back to your watercolor paper and trace your lettering with the masking fluid marker. Allow masking fluid to dry for about 5 to 10 minutes.

3. Splash your paper with watercolors! I put kraft paper under mine to protect my workspace from the mess. Tilt your paper to the side to make the watercolor drips. Load your paint brush with paint and gently flick or tap it with your finger to create extra paint splatters.

4. Allow your artwork to dry thoroughly. Once dry, gently rub the masking fluid off with your finger. Make sure to do this step within 24 hours of painting, or it might not come off so easily. Gently erase out any visible pencil marks, and then display your awesome artwork!

TIP!

Use this method to create DIY art prints, cards, stationery, and more!

MIXED MEDIA SIGN ✳

✳

I love mixed media art because anything goes! Show off your personal style!
I used a pallet style wood sign I picked up at the craft store, but a canvas would work really
well too. All my other supplies were things I already had on hand that I felt went well together.
I generally don't go into mixed media art with an overall plan. I just like to start,
add things at random, and see where it ends up! While planning is sometimes necessary,
it's really fun to just create mixed media art spontaneously.

SUPPLIES:

- Wood sign or canvas
- Assorted scrapbook papers and card stock
- Scissors
- Mod Podge®
- Craft glue
- Paintbrushes
- Book pages
- Acrylic paints
- Stickers
- Bubble wrap
- Silk/paper flowers
- Assorted office supplies (paper clips, binder clips, mini clothespin)

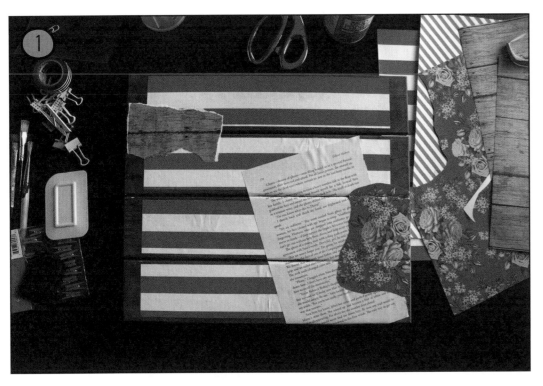

1. Glue your assorted papers to your sign or canvas. Try cutting and tearing the paper to add more character to your piece. I cut my striped, textured scrapbook paper into strips slightly smaller than each wood plank and then glued them to my wood sign. I added an old book page and some floral and wood scrapbook papers to my sign.

2. I painted a piece of bubble wrap with off-white paint and used it like a stamp to create texture on my sign.

3. Add stickers, and glue your office supplies to the sign at random. Paint over your sign with Mod Podge to seal it, and let it dry thoroughly. I picked pieces that I like to create with, work with, or that simply inspire me. I also added a mini clothespin to hang a hand-lettered note. The clothespin allows you to easily change out the quote, but you can glue your quote right to your sign or canvas if you prefer.

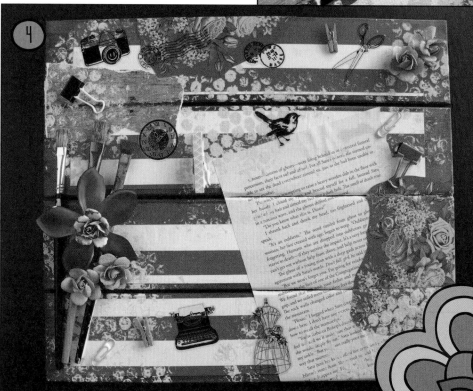

4. I glued on several silk and paper flowers.

5. Add some color with paint, and then attach your hand-lettering art. I added bright pink paint, and while I let the paint and glue dry, I wrote out the quote, "Work hard and be nice" on white card stock using brush calligraphy (with a Tombow Fudenosuke Soft Tip Brush Pen). I carefully tore the edges, and then glued it to a piece of teal card stock. Finally, I hung it on the mini clothespin. Hang it up and enjoy your artwork!

FLORAL LETTERING PRINT

Floral prints are one of my all-time favorite things to create with hand lettering! It is a lot simpler to create than it might look, and there are so many variations of beautiful artwork you can make with this style!

SUPPLIES:

- Sketch pad
- Pencil
- Eraser
- Black markers
- Markers, colored pencils, watercolors

1. Pick a phrase and sketch out some ideas. I used the phrase "Stop & Smell the Flowers."

2. Sketch your phrase in pencil on your sketch pad. A block lettering style works really well for these floral prints.

3. Trace over your lettering in marker. I used a fine-point Sharpie. Once dry, erase out your pencil lines, and draw several large flowers around your lettering.

4. Fill in the remaining open space with more artwork and doodles. Here are some ideas: small flowers, leaves, vines, hearts, dots, and butterflies.

Stop & Smell THE flowers

5. Add color with the medium of your choice!

WATERCOLOR LETTERING

Watercolors are an awesome medium because you don't need to be a pro for them to look pretty—they just do! Here are two different styles of working with watercolors. For these prints, I used the phrase "Honor Your Pace." What does that mean? Strive for progress, not perfection. The imperfections of hand-drawn lettering and art are part of the charm. Embrace your unique style and be proud of your work and your progress. In other words, *Honor Your Pace*.

SUPPLIES:

- Watercolor paper (I use cold-pressed Canson® Watercolor 140-lb.)
- Pencil/watercolor pencil
- Eraser
- Watercolors (I'm using the Kuretake Gansai Tambi® set. It's my favorite solid watercolor set!)
- Watercolor paintbrushes
- Water brush
- Black sumi ink

STYLE ONE STEPS:

1. Pick a phrase and sketch out some ideas. Draw the lettering in pencil (or watercolor pencil) in your watercolor pad. Faux Calligraphy and Block Lettering styles work really well—that's what I did for this print. Paint your lettering with watercolors. I used different rainbow colors for each letter. I used a really small 10/0 round paintbrush for the thin lines and a small angled brush for the thicker areas.

②

2. Let dry, then gently erase out any visible pencil lines.

honor YOUR pace

STYLE TWO STEPS:

1. Paint an abstract watercolor shape on your watercolor paper. I used two colors in the blue-green family.

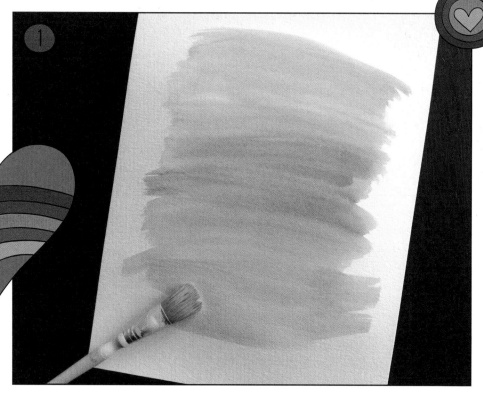

2. When dry, use a water brush filled with 50% water and 50% black ink to add your lettering! You can also use a watercolor paintbrush, such as a No. 4 round, to achieve the same look.

honor YOUR pace

ILLUSTRATED PRINT

Adding illustration is such a great way to add character and personal style to your lettering. We've already touched on this with the floral lettering piece, but the ways to add illustration to your work are pretty much endless. For my piece, I used the quote "Do what makes you oh so happy." I added a vine frame with heart corners, a banner, some line art, several styles of lettering, and hearts.

SUPPLIES:

- Sketch pad
- Pencil
- Eraser
- Colored pencils, markers, etc.

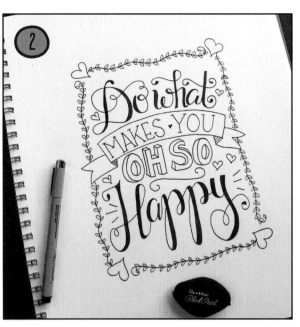

1. Sketch out ideas on scrap paper to get a feel for how you want to lay out your lettering and illustration. Once you're happy with the layout, move to your sketch pad and sketch your chosen design in pencil. I like to draw an 8" x 10" frame to keep my print a size that can be framed.

2. Trace with a fine-point black marker.

Do what MAKES YOU OH SO Happy

SHAPE LETTERING PRINT

Shape lettering is a great way to stretch your lettering skills. Making a quote fit into a particular shape can be a challenge, but it's a fun one! For this example, I used a heart and the Rumi quote, "Let the beauty of what you love be what you do." Just for fun, I also added a bunch of doodles around my heart-shaped quote! When you select a quote, be sure it goes along with the theme of the shape you've chosen.

SUPPLIES:

- Sketch pad
- Pencil
- Eraser
- Colored pencils, markers, etc.

1. Sketch out ideas on scrap paper to get a feel for how you want to lay out your lettering within the shape. Once you're happy with the layout, move to your sketch pad and sketch your chosen design in pencil.

2. Trace with a fine-point black marker.

3. Let dry, erase pencil lines, and add color!

Let the BEAUTY of what you LOVE be what you do. —RUMI!

TIP!

Here are a few more fun shapes to try lettering within:

Globe • Butterfly
Arrow • Flag • Whale

GEL PEN ART

This exercise is about exploring a new medium for lettering. Gel pens look so cool on dark papers. I often use black paper, but for this quote I decided on a dark blue paper. It's helpful to keep a second scrap piece of the same color paper nearby so you can test your gel pen colors to make sure you like them.

For this exercise, try to incorporate the lessons and lettering styles we've done so far. The trick with gel pens is patience. Go nice and slow to get thick gel lines, and allow each color to dry as you work so you don't smear anything. Note that gel pens take a bit longer to dry than many other mediums.

SUPPLIES:
- Dark card stock
- Pencil
- Eraser
- Gel pens

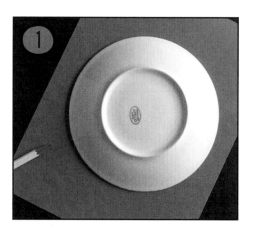

1. Draw a circle on your page in pencil. I often grab a household object to trace for a perfect circle.

2. Use your gel pens to doodle flowers and leaves all around the circle.

3. Lightly sketch in your lettering, and then go over it with a white gel pen. Add more illustrations to fill space and create balance. If you look closely at my original wreath and final piece, you can see where I've done this in my print. Let dry completely and then gently erase out any visible pencil lines.

BE THE DESIGNER

This section is filled with projects that are all about having fun! When I was in design school, we had a ton of projects like this, and I loved doing them. With these projects, you'll apply all of the lettering styles and skills you've learned so far and really shine as a designer. For each project, I will give you a prompt (or a few prompts), and then you will design the lettering and illustration.

Typography and design are all around you! As you walk through stores, start paying attention to the amazing typographic and artistic designs on products. I snap pictures of my favorites with my phone to print and put in my inspiration journal.
Now let's get to work designing!

GREETING CARDS

A greeting card company has asked to you design a trio of birthday greeting cards—two vertical and one horizontal. They want you to mix lettering and illustration, but they really love your style so any other details, such as theme and color, are totally up to you!

GIFT TAGS

Your neighbor is a local shop owner, and she loves your work! She would like you to design a set of everyday gift tags she can sell in her shop. She has given you a template of tag styles. All you have to do is add your lettering and illustrations.

Here are some ideas for what to put on your gift tags:

Just for You

Handmade with Love

Enjoy!

To: / From:

Love

Thank you

Thanks!

Enjoy!

Hello

XOXO

NOTE CARD SET

The greeting card company loved your work on the birthday cards, so now they would like you to design a set of four note cards. They would like it to be a mixed set: two thank you cards and two everyday note cards. The cards will be sold as a set, so the overall look and color scheme should be similar. (In my example below, the overall look and color scheme vary to give you some inspiration and ideas).

T-SHIRT DESIGN

A local clothing company has asked to you design a set of t-shirts for the whole family for their spring line. There are four shirts you will need to design: one men's, one women's, and two children's (one masculine design and one feminine).

They would like the men's shirt to be bold and simple, the women's shirt to use pretty script lettering with flourishing, and the kids' designs to be fun and playful. The text for all four shirts will be "Wild & Free." inspired by the Henry David Thoreau quote, "All good things are wild and free." Any other details are up to you!

NOTEBOOK COVER

A local specialty paper goods company has asked to you design an inspirational notebook cover. They'd like you use bright, happy colors and the phrase "Keep going! You've got this!" You can use lettering or a combination of lettering and illustration in the cover design.

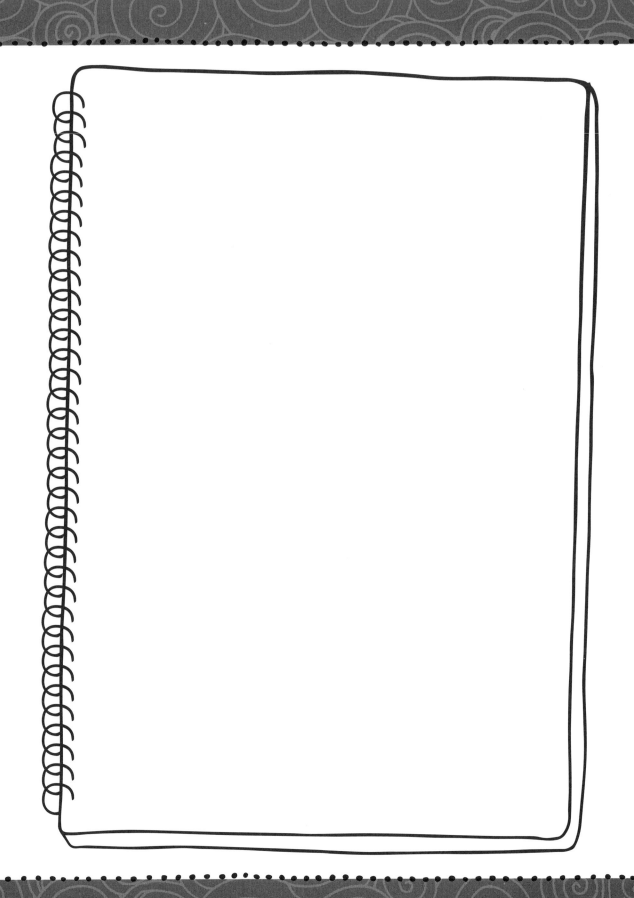

LOGO

Congratulations! Your design work is really taking off. It's time to create a logo for your company. Using your name, design a hand-lettered logo for your design company. Since you are your brand, it's great to have your name as part of your company. It also gives it a personal touch. I've provided examples of my own logo, and one I designed for a friend.

My logo conveys my name, my lettering style, and that I'm a designer. The pink watercolor paint also conveys that my style is feminine and that I'm an artist. I used faux calligraphy to design my logo's lettering.

My friend Alicia wanted her logo to incorporate her business name and to be hand-lettered, feminine, and a symbol of sewing. I used brush calligraphy (with a Tombow Fudenosuke) to design her logo's lettering.

Usually when I design a logo for a client, I send them around three designs to pick from. I encourage you to do the same for yourself. Design three logos and then pick one. You can even ask family and friends to weigh in on which design they like best.

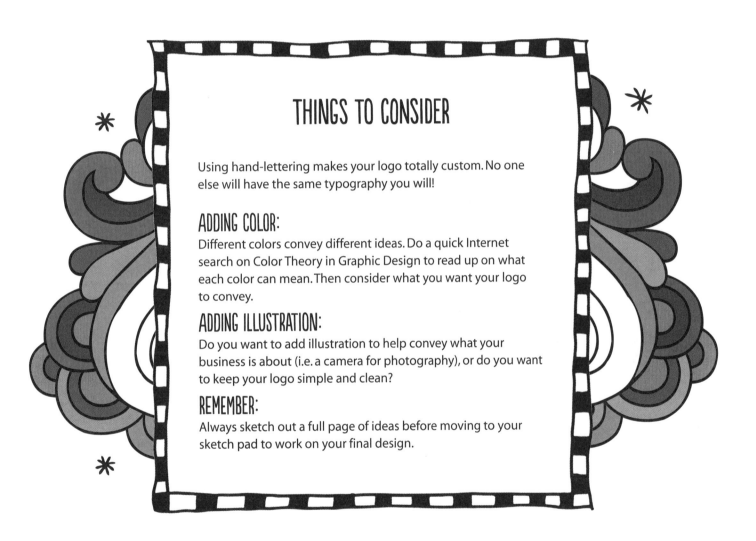

THINGS TO CONSIDER

Using hand-lettering makes your logo totally custom. No one else will have the same typography you will!

ADDING COLOR:
Different colors convey different ideas. Do a quick Internet search on Color Theory in Graphic Design to read up on what each color can mean. Then consider what you want your logo to convey.

ADDING ILLUSTRATION:
Do you want to add illustration to help convey what your business is about (i.e. a camera for photography), or do you want to keep your logo simple and clean?

REMEMBER:
Always sketch out a full page of ideas before moving to your sketch pad to work on your final design.

CUPCAKE TOPPERS

A local party planner is planning a sweet shoppe themed party. She has asked you to design some fun cupcake toppers for the party. The text for the toppers is "Stay sweet" and the colors should be inspired by bright candy. You need to design three to five different options for her to choose from.

STAY Sweet

TOTE BAG

A national grocery store chain is having a design contest. The winner's design will be featured on all the store's reusable tote bags. Anything goes as far as the style of the design, but the text should say, "Make the world a pretty place." Create your entry on the blank tote bag.

BOOK COVER

A family friend has written her first book, and she has asked you to design the cover. She would like it to be simple, bright, and fun. Your hand-lettered typography using the title "It Takes All Types" should be the star of the cover.

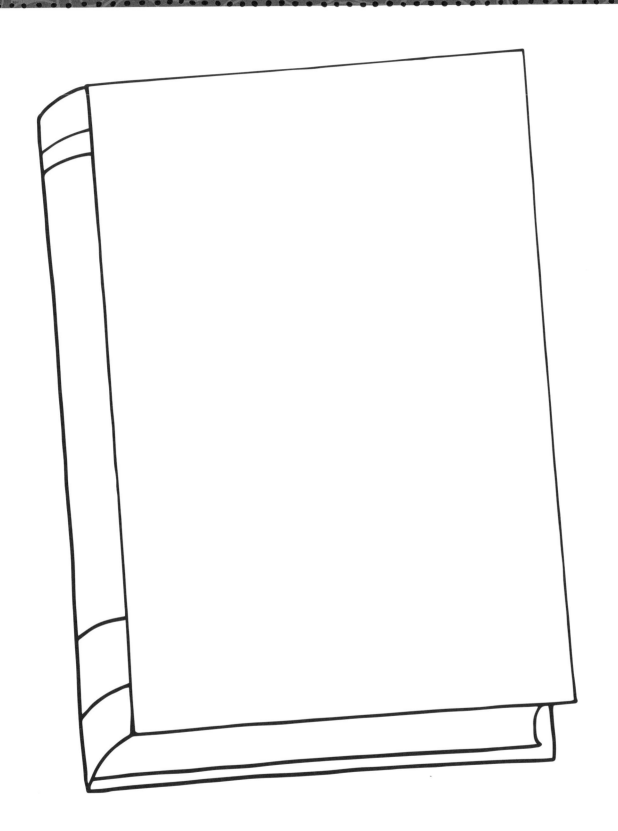

COFFEE MUG

A national gift shop has asked you to design a mug for their new motivational line. They would like it to be trendy and bright in color, but you have a lot of freedom to get as creative as you'd like with the mug colors and lettering. The text for your mug design is "Wake Up & Be Awesome." Design three options to present.

COLORING PAGES

In this section, I've provided some designed coloring pages for you to enjoy and color. Take what you have learned throughout this book to turn these pages into your own awesome hand-lettered artwork!

Do what MAKES YOU OH SO Happy